VIOLA
101 JAZZ SONGS

Available for
FLUTE, CLARINET, ALTO SAX, TENOR SAX, TRUMPET,
HORN, TROMBONE, VIOLIN, VIOLA, CELLO

ISBN 978-1-4950-2345-3

HAL•LEONARD®
CORPORATION
7777 W. BLUEMOUND RD. P.O. BOX 13819 MILWAUKEE, WI 53213

Visit Hal Leonard Online at
www.halleonard.com

CONTENTS

ALL OF ME

VIOLA

Words and Music by SEYMOUR SIMONS
and GERALD MARKS

ALL THE THINGS YOU ARE

VIOLA

Lyrics by OSCAR HAMMERSTEIN II
Music by JEROME KERN

APRIL IN PARIS

VIOLA

Words by E.Y. "YIP" HARBURG
Music by VERNON DUKE

AUTUMN IN NEW YORK

VIOLA

Words and Music by
VERNON DUKE

AUTUMN LEAVES

VIOLA

English Lyric by JOHNNY MERCER
French Lyric by JACQUES PREVERT
Music by JOSEPH KOSMA

BEWITCHED

VIOLA

Words by LORENZ HART
Music by RICHARD RODGERS

BEYOND THE SEA

Lyrics by JACK LAWRENCE
Music by CHARLES TRENET and ALBERT LASRY
Original French Lyric to "La Mer" by CHARLES TRENET

VIOLA

THE BLUE ROOM

VIOLA

Words by LORENZ HART
Music by RICHARD RODGERS

BLUE SKIES

VIOLA

Words and Music by
IRVING BERLIN

BLUESETTE

VIOLA

Words by NORMAN GIMBEL
Music by JEAN THIELEMANS

BODY AND SOUL

VIOLA

Words by EDWARD HEYMAN,
ROBERT SOUR and FRANK EYTON
Music by JOHN GREEN

BUT BEAUTIFUL

VIOLA

Words by JOHNNY BURKE
Music by JIMMY VAN HEUSEN

CAN'T HELP LOVIN' DAT MAN

VIOLA

Lyrics by OSCAR HAMMERSTEIN II
Music by JEROME KERN

CARAVAN

VIOLA

Words and Music by DUKE ELLINGTON,
IRVING MILLS and JUAN TIZOL

CHARADE

VIOLA

By HENRY MANCINI

CHEEK TO CHEEK

VIOLA

Words and Music by
IRVING BERLIN

COME RAIN OR COME SHINE

VIOLA

Words by JOHNNY MERCER
Music by HAROLD ARLEN

DANCING ON THE CEILING

VIOLA

Words by LORENZ HART
Music by RICHARD RODGERS

DEARLY BELOVED

VIOLA

Music by JEROME KERN
Words by JOHNNY MERCER

DO NOTHIN' TILL YOU HEAR FROM ME

VIOLA

Words and Music by DUKE ELLINGTON
and BOB RUSSELL

DON'T GET AROUND MUCH ANYMORE

VIOLA

Words and Music by DUKE ELLINGTON
and BOB RUSSELL

DREAMSVILLE

VIOLA

By HENRY MANCINI

FALLING IN LOVE WITH LOVE

VIOLA

Words by LORENZ HART
Music by RICHARD RODGERS

A FINE ROMANCE

VIOLA

Words by DOROTHY FIELDS
Music by JEROME KERN

FLY ME TO THE MOON
(In Other Words)

VIOLA

Words and Music by
BART HOWARD

GEORGIA ON MY MIND

VIOLA

Words by STUART GORRELL
Music by HOAGY CARMICHAEL

HERE'S THAT RAINY DAY

VIOLA

Words by JOHNNY BURKE
Music by JIMMY VAN HEUSEN

HERE'S TO LIFE

VIOLA

Music by ARTIE BUTLER
Lyrics by PHYLLIS MOLINARY

HONEYSUCKLE ROSE

VIOLA

Words by ANDY RAZAF
Music by THOMAS "FATS" WALLER

HOW DEEP IS THE OCEAN
(How High Is the Sky)

VIOLA

Words and Music by
IRVING BERLIN

HOW INSENSITIVE
(Insensatez)

Music by ANTONIO CARLOS JOBIM
Original Words by VINICIUS DE MORAES
English Words by NORMAN GIMBEL

VIOLA

Medium Bossa Nova

I CAN'T GET STARTED

VIOLA

Words by IRA GERSHWIN
Music by VERNON DUKE

I COULD WRITE A BOOK

VIOLA

Words by LORENZ HART
Music by RICHARD RODGERS

I GOT IT BAD AND THAT AIN'T GOOD

VIOLA

Words by PAUL FRANCIS WEBSTER
Music by DUKE ELLINGTON

I'LL REMEMBER APRIL

VIOLA

Words and Music by PAT JOHNSTON,
DON RAYE AND GENE DE PAUL

I'M BEGINNING TO SEE THE LIGHT

VIOLA

Words and Music by DON GEORGE, JOHNNY HODGES, DUKE ELLINGTON and HARRY JAMES

Medium Bounce

I'VE GOT THE WORLD ON A STRING

VIOLA

Words by TED KOEHLER
Music by HAROLD ARLEN

IF I WERE A BELL

VIOLA

By FRANK LOESSER

IMAGINATION

VIOLA

Words by JOHNNY BURKE
Music by JIMMY VAN HEUSEN

IN A SENTIMEMTAL MOOD

VIOLA

By DUKE ELLINGTON

IN THE WEE SMALL HOURS OF THE MORNING

VIOLA

Words by BOB HILLIARD
Music by DAVID MANN

INDIANA
(Back Home Again in Indiana)

VIOLA

Words by BALLARD MacDONALD
Music by JAMES F. HANLEY

ISN'T IT ROMANTIC?

VIOLA

Words by LORENZ HART
Music by RICHARD RODGERS

IT COULD HAPPEN TO YOU

VIOLA

Words by JOHNNY BURKE
Music by JAMES VAN HEUSEN

IT DON'T MEAN A THING
(If It Ain't Got That Swing)

VIOLA

Words and Music by DUKE ELLINGTON
and IRVING MILLS

IT MIGHT AS WELL BE SPRING

VIOLA

Lyrics by OSCAR HAMMERSTEIN II
Music by RICHARD RODGERS

THE LADY IS A TRAMP

VIOLA

Words by LORENZ HART
Music by RICHARD RODGERS

LAZY RIVER

VIOLA

Words and Music by HOAGY CARMICHAEL
and SIDNEY ARODIN

LET THERE BE LOVE

VIOLA

Lyric by IAN GRANT
Music by LIONEL RAND

LIKE SOMEONE IN LOVE

VIOLA

Words by JOHNNY BURKE
Music by JIMMY VAN HEUSEN

LITTLE GIRL BLUE

VIOLA

Words by LORENZ HART
Music by RICHARD RODGERS

LONG AGO (AND FAR AWAY)

VIOLA

Words by IRA GERSHWIN
Music by JEROME KERN

LOVER, COME BACK TO ME

VIOLA

Lyrics by OSCAR HAMMERSTEIN II
Music by SIGMUND ROMBERG

LULLABY OF BIRDLAND

VIOLA

Words by GEORGE DAVID WEISS
Music by GEORGE SHEARING

LULLABY OF THE LEAVES

VIOLA

Words by JOE YOUNG
Music by BERNICE PETKERE

MANHATTAN

VIOLA

Words by LORENZ HART
Music by RICHARD RODGERS

MEDITATION
(Meditação)

VIOLA

Music by ANTONIO CARLOS JOBIM
Original Words by NEWTON MENDONÇA
English Words by NORMAN GIMBEL

Medium Bossa Nova

MIDNIGHT SUN

VIOLA

Words and Music by LIONEL HAMPTON,
SONNY BURKE and JOHNNY MERCER

MISTY

VIOLA

Music by ERROLL GARNER

MOOD INDIGO

VIOLA

Words and Music by DUKE ELLINGTON,
IRVING MILLS and ALBANY BIGARD

MOONLIGHT IN VERMONT

VIOLA

Words by JOHN BLACKBURN
Music by KARL SUESSDORF

MORE THAN YOU KNOW

VIOLA

Words by WILLIAM ROSE and EDWARD ELISCU
Music by VINCENT YOUMANS

MY HEART STOOD STILL

VIOLA

Words by LORENZ HART
Music by RICHARD RODGERS

MY OLD FLAME

VIOLA

Words and Music by ARTHUR JOHNSTON
and SAM COSLOW

MY ONE AND ONLY LOVE

VIOLA

Words by ROBERT MELLIN
Music by GUY WOOD

MY ROMANCE

VIOLA

Words by LORENZ HART
Music by RICHARD RODGERS

MY SHIP

VIOLA

Words by IRA GERSHWIN
Music by KURT WEILL

THE NEARNESS OF YOU

VIOLA

Words by NED WASHINGTON
Music by HOAGY CARMICHAEL

A NIGHT IN TUNISIA

VIOLA

By JOHN "DIZZY" GILLESPIE
and FRANK PAPARELLI

Moderately fast Swing

ON GREEN DOLPHIN STREET

Viola

Lyrics by NED WASHINGTON
Music by BRONISLAU KAPER

ONE NOTE SAMBA
(Samba de uma nota so)

VIOLA

Original Lyrics by NEWTON MENDONÇA
English Lyrics by ANTONIO CARLOS JOBIM
Music by ANTONIO CARLOS JOBIM

Medium Bossa Nova

PICK YOURSELF UP

VIOLA

Words by DOROTHY FIELDS
Music by JEROME KERN

POLKA DOTS AND MOONBEAMS

VIOLA

Words by JOHNNY BURKE
Music by JIMMY VAN HEUSEN

QUIET NIGHTS OF QUIET STARS
(Corcovado)

VIOLA

English Words by GENE LEES
Original Words and Music by ANTONIO CARLOS JOBIM

Medium Bossa Nova

SATIN DOLL

VIOLA

By DUKE ELLINGTON

Medium Swing

SKYLARK

VIOLA

Words by JOHNNY MERCER
Music by HOAGY CARMICHAEL

SO NICE
(Summer Samba)

VIOLA

Original Words and Music by MARCOS VALLE
and PAULO SERGIO VALLE
English Words by NORMAN GIMBEL

Medium Bossa Nova

SOPHISTICATED LADY

VIOLA

Words and Music by DUKE ELLINGTON,
IRVING MILLS and MITCHELL PARISH

SPEAK LOW

VIOLA

Words by OGDEN NASH
Music by KURT WEILL

STELLA BY STARLIGHT

VIOLA

Words by NED WASHINGTON
Music by VICTOR YOUNG

STOMPIN' AT THE SAVOY

VIOLA

By BENNY GOODMAN,
EDGAR SAMPSON and CHICK WEBB

Bright Swing

STORMY WEATHER
(Keeps Rainin' All the Time)

VIOLA

Lyric by TED KOEHLER
Music by HAROLD ARLEN

Moderately slow, with a lilt

A SUNDAY KIND OF LOVE

VIOLA

Words and Music by LOUIS PRIMA, ANITA NYE LEONARD, STANLEY RHODES and BARBARA BELLE

TANGERINE

VIOLA

Words by JOHNNY MERCER
Music by VICTOR SCHERTZINGER

THERE'S A SMALL HOTEL

VIOLA

Words by LORENZ HART
Music by RICHARD RODGERS

THESE FOOLISH THINGS (REMIND ME OF YOU)

VIOLA

Words by HOLT MARVELL
Music by JACK STRACHEY

Medium Swing

THE THINGS WE DID LAST SUMMER

VIOLA

Words by SAMMY CAHN
Music by JULE STYNE

This Can't Be Love

VIOLA

Words by LORENZ HART
Music by RICHARD RODGERS

THOU SWELL

VIOLA

Words by LORENZ HART
Music by RICHARD RODGERS

UNFORGETTABLE

VIOLA

Words and Music by
IRVING GORDON

THE VERY THOUGHT OF YOU

VIOLA

Words and Music by
RAY NOBLE

With a slow, easy Swing

WATCH WHAT HAPPENS

Music by MICHEL LEGRAND
Original French Text by JACQUES DEMY
English Lyrics by NORMAN GIMBEL

VIOLA

WAVE

VIOLA

Words and Music by
ANTONIO CARLOS JOBIM

THE WAY YOU LOOK TONIGHT

VIOLA

Words by DOROTHY FIELDS
Music by JEROME KERN

WHAT'LL I DO

VIOLA

Words and Music by
IRVING BERLIN

WILLOW WEEP FOR ME

VIOLA

Words and Music by
ANN RONELL

WITCHCRAFT

VIOLA

Music by CY COLEMAN
Lyrics by CAROLYN LEIGH

YESTERDAYS

VIOLA

Words by OTTO HARBACH
Music by JEROME KERN

YOU ARE TOO BEAUTIFUL

VIOLA

Words by LORENZ HART
Music by RICHARD RODGERS

YOU BROUGHT A NEW KIND OF LOVE TO ME

VIOLA

Words and Music by SAMMY FAIN,
IRVING KAHAL and PIERRE NORMAN

YOU DON'T KNOW WHAT LOVE IS

VIOLA

Words and Music by DON RAYE
and GENE DePAUL